Jesus
and
you

David Marshall

First published 2009

© 2009

British Library Cataloguing in Publication Data. A catalogue record for this book is available from the British Library.

ISBN 978-1-906381-55-4

Published by Autumn House, Grantham, Lincolnshire.

Printed in Thailand.

Unless otherwise indicated, all Scripture references are taken from the *New International Version* (Hodder and Stoughton). Other versions used, indicated by initials, are:
KJV = *King James Version*
JBP = *The New Testament in Modern English* by J. B. Phillips (Collins)
MGE = *The Message: The Bible in Contemporary Language* (NavPress)
NKJV = *New King James Version* (Thomas Nelson)

Jesus

is God spelling Himself out
in language that man can
understand.
S. D. Gordon

Dear Alisha

My prayer for you is "Godliness"
that you will conquer nations
for God in Jesus Christ.

lots of love
xxx   Nanny Lightfoot

Most men are notable for one conspicuous virtue or grace. Moses for meekness. Job for patience. John for love.

But in Jesus you find everything.
J. Oswald Sanders

One solitary life

Here is a man who was born
in an obscure village, the
Child of a peasant woman.
He worked in a carpenter's
shop until He was thirty, and
then for three years He was
an itinerant preacher.

He never wrote a book. He never held an office. He never owned a home. He never had a family. He never went to college. He never put His foot inside a really big city. He never travelled two hundred miles from the place where He was born. He never did one of the things that usually accompany greatness.

He had no credentials but Himself. He had nothing to do with this world except the naked power of His Divine manhood. While still a young man, the tide of popular opinion turned against Him. He was turned over to His enemies. He went through the mockery of a trial.

He was nailed to a Cross between two thieves. His executioners gambled for the only piece of property He had on earth while He was dying – and that was His coat. When He was dead He was taken down and laid in a borrowed grave through the pity of a friend. Such was His human life.

He rose from the dead.

Nineteen wide centuries
have come and gone
and today He is the
centrepiece of the
human race and the
Leader of the column
of progress.

I am well within the mark when
I say that all the armies that ever
marched, and all the navies that
were ever built, and all the
parliaments that ever sat, and
all the kings that ever reigned,
put together, have not affected
the life of man upon the earth as
powerfully as has that One
Solitary Life.

*Attributed to various people but
most credibly to Phillips Brooks.*

Who was he?

He lived in a country with a population of less than half a million. By any standards it was a tiny country; a hundred and fifty miles from end to end, fifty miles across.

His story takes off in the most cosmopolitan province of that tiny country. . . .

Traffic from 'the four
corners' passed close
by the town where
he was reared. Roman
occupation was the
great issue of the age.
His home-town hills
harboured freedom
fighters. . . .

In the year of his birth there was a widespread belief common to many cultures (Roman, Greek, Persian, Hebrew) that a world Deliverer would arise. But if he was that Deliverer few saw him as such.

This was not surprising. He was born in an outhouse, not a palace. Some sniggered at the circumstances of his birth. His training was of a practical nature; he received no formal education. When he left home he lived rough out of doors.

He had the capacity to
inspire loyalty, but knew few,
if any, of the 'right people'.
He shunned popularity and
refused political position.

Short of a 'rise and rise'
to fame and fortune, to the
image-conscious his career
was a saga of missed
opportunities.

When his words of wisdom
began to collide with
expectation, he lost all
but a nucleus of his original
followers. And one of them
betrayed him.

Early thirties, still in his
prime, he was arrested,
suffered a sham trial and
was subjected to a criminal's
death.

The really remarkable thing about the Jesus story is that what was meant to have been the end – was actually only the beginning.

Three days after his execution a persistent rumour ran through the streets of his country's capital: he had come to life again! In circumstances in which they could very easily have been proved wrong the nucleus of his followers preached: his tomb is empty, we have seen and talked to him, he is risen.

His followers had cowered in corners behind bolted doors after his execution, but they now stood fearlessly before the Supreme Court of the land, heads erect, and said: 'The Man you put to death is alive. He is God's Son. We are his witnesses.'

The nucleus of the followers of Jesus became the most powerful force known to history.

Time itself is measured by the life of Jesus on Earth. Each year is given the stamp of his authority, *Anno Domini*, the year of our Lord.

Napoleon, exiled on St Helena, remarked: 'Alexander, Caesar, Charlemagne and I founded empires. But on what did the creations of our genius rest? Upon force. Jesus alone founded His empire on love, and to this very day millions would die for Him.'

From the story of his birth, life, ministry, death and resurrection, centuries of men have derived the moral, spiritual and intellectual creativity out of which has come everything great (*truly* great) in our art, architecture and music.

The Jesus story has illuminated thousands of the greatest minds. The number of individuals who claim and have claimed that their lives have been changed, rebuilt, transformed by him is utterly beyond our powers of computation.

C. S. Lewis said that Jesus was either a charlatan or he was exactly what he said he was. Certainly his claims do not allow us to take an in-between position. 'The claims Jesus made for Himself offer us two alternative beliefs. Either He was completely mad, a megalomaniac caught in the toils of His own deceptions, or He was God come to live then die that centuries of prophecy might be fulfilled and that man might be redeemed, reborn and transformed.'

Logic dictates:
Either he never was,
or he still is.

Which? He was mad,
or bad, or God.

And no one is saying
he was mad or bad. . . .

At the turn of the eras (BC/AD) and on the tick of prophecy, a thin cry pierced the blue cold of midnight in royal David's overcrowded city: Bethlehem. A child born amid the deep and dreamless sleep of this tiny town wherein the hopes and fears of all the years were met . . .

. . . Joseph and heavily pregnant Mary had travelled sixty miles from Nazareth so that in the fullness of God's time the Son of the Highest might be born.

There was no room for them at the inn so Jesus was born in a place where beasts took shelter.

The Messiah's first bed was among the sharp straws of an animal feeding trough: the manger. Shepherds and wise men came to visit. But the many-splendoured birth was ignored by all the 'right people'.

The shepherds and the wise men saw in the baby a wonder that outshone the seven wonders of their world. The Living God had enshrined his glory in human flesh – suffused with blood, structured by bones, intertwined with veins, threaded with nerves.

And here he was: in a manger.

'The Word was made flesh . . .'

God did not reveal Himself in the rumble of an earthquake or in a mushroom cloud; but in the simple features of a human countenance. Our gaze is all transfixed – and faith is leaping out to grasp Him.

G. T. Bull

Holy God was wholly flesh; and wrapped in swaddling clothes.

Eyes accustomed to observing the earth from end to end could not focus on his mother's face. Hands that fashioned moon and stars could not grasp his mother's finger. The Voice 'that spoke and it was done' was inarticulate and speechless.

Jesus Christ:

The meeting place of time and eternity, the blending of deity and humanity, the junction of Heaven and Earth.

Jesus was raised in the Nazareth carpenter's shop where, like all other well-trained Hebrew youth, he had learned his father's trade.

'No other God have
I but Thee;
Born in a manger,
died on a tree.'
Martin Luther

When Jesus tore himself away from the carpenter's shop, he went down to the Jordan to be baptised by John. Before Jesus ('holy, harmless, undefiled') John hesitated. Jesus replied, *'Let it be so now; it is proper for us to do this to fulfil all righteousness.'*
(Matthew 3:13-15.)

The Jordan was a symbol. It originated in the vast acreages of undented snow on the summits of Mount Hermon. The beauty of its earlier course to, through and beyond Galilee was symbolic of man as the Creator had made him: in his own image. But the troubled waters where John baptised were hurrying on to the Sea of Death and represented death-deserving, sinful man with whom Jesus had come to identify himself.

The most urgent
problem each one of
us will ever have to
face is the one in our
mirror. The fundamental
problems we face are
sin, sorrow, guilt,
judgement and death.
And basic to all is the
sin problem.

Sin is a reality that breaks hearts, blights homes, robs Heaven. Sin is a madness in the brain, a poison in the heart. It promises nectar; it gives gall.

But there is no heart without it.

Tackling the sin problem requires more than a change of environment; more than education or psychology can offer. The sinner needs more than the outward trappings of religion.
Man needs power from without to cleanse him.
He needs power from without to give him new life.
He is dependent upon Another, even One who slept the sleep of death – and, awoken from it, destroyed the power of death.

'God so loved the world that he gave his one and only Son, that whoever believes in him shall not perish but have eternal life. For God did not send his Son into the world to condemn the world, but to save the world through him.' The words of Jesus in John's gospel chapter 3, verses 16 and 17.

*The words look,
believe – and be
saved!*

That is Gospel Truth!

John 3:16 is the greatest verse in Scripture. Why? Because it concerns the greatest Giver: God. Because it mentions the greatest thing in the world: love. Because it refers to the greatest group it is possible to love: the world. Because it mentions the greatest evidence of love: giving.

Because it enshrines the greatest gift ever bestowed: God's only Son. Because it includes the greatest invitation: whosoever. Because the only condition mentioned is one of the greatest simplicity: believing. Because it promises the greatest of rewards: everlasting life.

If our greatest need had been
   information,
   God would have sent us a
   teacher.
If our greatest need had been
   technology,
   God would have sent us a
   scientist.
If our greatest need had been
   money,
   God would have sent us an
economist.

If our greatest need had been pleasure,
  God would have sent us an entertainer.
But our greatest need was forgiveness,
  So God sent us a Saviour!

Charles R. Swindoll,
The Grace Awakening

Jesus came to the Feast of the Passover in AD31 to offer himself as the Paschal Lamb; 'the Lamb of God that taketh away the sin of the world'. He had come to offer himself as the sacrifice:

Not for one man or
a select few, a Chosen
People, but as a
ransom for all
mankind, always.
He said, *'I, when I
am lifted up from the
earth, will draw all
men to myself. . . .'*
(John 12:32.)

Caesar might dazzle mankind, as Caesars in their different configurations have continued to do, but the worship a Caesar demands, in the end, curdles because a poor carpenter from Nazareth ironically insisted that Caesar's bills can be paid in Caesar's coinage . . .

. . . whereas what is due to God is everything we do and are and can hope to be. The sacrifice Jesus came to give was to enable man to give himself to God washed clean of sin by the blood of the Paschal Lamb, covered with the righteousness of the One lifted up on Calvary's Cross.

The enemies of Jesus said, 'This man receives sinners!' They spoke the truth! Indeed, without knowing it, they expressed the core of the Christian Gospel. *'Whoever comes to me I will never drive away'* (John 6:37), Jesus said. No one who comes to Christ is ever refused.

Jesus was the Living Water.

To receive Living Water the only qualification necessary was thirst.

The last invitation of Scripture reads: 'Whoever is thirsty, let him come; and whoever wishes, let him take the free gift of the water of life.' Revelation 22:17.

Jesus stands absolutely alone in history; in teaching, in example, in character, an exception, a marvel, and he is himself the evidence of Christianity.

Jesus authenticates himself.

Oceans of paint, acres of canvas, whole mountains of stone and marble, miles of film and billions of words have been expended on the life of Jesus.

Are you so free of the sickness of sin that you can afford to reject out of hand his offer of healing and forgiveness?

A new convert had a strange
dream. He was trapped down
a very deep well in the night.
He looked up and saw a single
star shining far above him.
When he looked to its silver
light, it took hold of him and
lifted him up. When he looked
down, he began to go down.
He found that by simply
keeping his eye on that star,
he rose out of the well until
his foot stood on firm ground.

A. T. Pierson said: 'That dream was a parable. Get your eyes off yourself and on your Saviour, get them off your disease and on your Physician. . . . Now and here, turn your eyes to the Lord Jesus.'

Crusading atheist Arnold Toynbee wrote, ' Find the body of that Jew, and Christianity crumbles into ruins.'

No one ever has. No grave in the world claims one bone of the body of Jesus Christ.

Why?

He *is* risen!

Death died at the birth of that first Easter day. That morning it surrendered dominion, was led captive and humbled, made as it were a shadow to flee before the Light shining in the darkness. Because Christ died and rose again we may die to a sin-centred life and rise again to a new life.

John, who led the heartbroken mother of Jesus from the scene of his crucifixion, lived into old age. But, in exile, his hair white, John could not forget the thrill of what he had *'heard . . . and . . . handled of the Word of life'* (1 John 1:1, KJV).

John wanted, before it was too late, to set down on paper his recollections of Jesus. As he took up his quill pen he was for a moment carried away. Once more he saw the three crosses on that dreadful Friday. He wrote: *'And we beheld his glory . . . as of the only begotten of the Father.'*

John wrote of Jesus, '*He came unto his own, and his own received him not. But as many as received him, to them gave he power to become the sons of God, even to them that believe on his name.*'
(John 1:14, 11, 12, KJV.)

The glory of the Cross was the glory of the finished redemption for as many as received him. As the dense darkness lifted from Calvary these words sounded above the confusion of men's voices: *'It is finished.'*

The price for sin had been paid. The destructive power of sin had been broken.

The only thing needed for someone to prick the bubble of early Christianity was for them to walk a distance no greater than that from Hyde Park Corner to Marble Arch; that is, if the tomb of Jesus was *not* empty.

The tomb of Jesus was empty. Friends and enemies knew it. It was beyond dispute. So no one disputed it.

In the years ahead the cause of the risen Christ was unstoppable. Of course, there were those who *tried* to stop it – by fire, stoning, sword, the various forms of judicial murder. But one of Christianity's foremost detractors, Saul of Tarsus, became the champion of Christ's cause.

Saul, who became Paul, encountered the risen Christ on the way to wipe out Christianity in Damascus. His resistance crumbled on the instant of the encounter.

Imprisoned towards the end of his life, Paul wrote, *'I am not ashamed of the gospel, because it is the power of God for the salvation of everyone who believes.'* (Romans 1:16.)

The risen Lord appeared to various groups at different times before the ascension, on one occasion to five hundred at once, most of whom were still alive twenty years later to testify to the fact.
(1 Corinthians 15:6.)

The fact and power of the resurrection launched 'a winged thunderbolt of everlasting enthusiasm' (G. K. Chesterton). From Jerusalem, an intensely heated centre of burning zeal, a vast field of lava was thrown to the limits of the Roman world.

But the men at the centre
of all this had fled from
Gethsemane! One had denied
his Lord with oaths! All had
spent the period between
crucifixion and resurrection
holed up behind closed doors.

The resurrection made the
difference.

The very same men who hid away while the crucifixion was happening, for fear of their lives, preached the resurrection before vast crowds, converting thousands. The empty tomb served as a visual aid to their preaching: a fact, there, present, accessible, proof and no doubt.

The resurrection had caught these men completely unprepared. *Afterwards* they recalled his promises. But at the time, far from inventing the resurrection, they themselves, against their inclinations, had to be persuaded that it was a fact.

At first fear gripped the disciples on Easter Sunday. That is why the first words of the Easter angels were: ' "Do not be afraid." ' They 'hurried away from the tomb, afraid', 'trembling and bewildered, [they] fled from the tomb', 'in their fright . . . bowed down', 'they were startled and frightened, thinking they saw a ghost.' Matthew 28:5, 8; Mark 16:8; Luke 24:5, 37-39.

Even when the resurrection
facts were irrefutable the
disciples hardly dared believe.

As the female disciples
approached the tomb of
Jesus at first light on Sunday
morning they worried about
the stone 'which was very
large' (Mark 16:1-4).

These women did not expect a resurrection. Far from it. Their analysis of what they saw was practical, clinical, and common sense: ' *"They have taken the Lord out of the tomb."* ' (John 20:2.) Two disciples on the road to Emmaus were aware of the women's testimony and dismissed it with the words: ' *"Him they did not see."* ' (Luke 24:22-24.)

Peter left the tomb 'wondering to himself what had happened' (Luke 24:12). The others *'did not understand from Scripture that Jesus had to rise from the dead'. 'They did not believe the women, because their words seemed to them like nonsense.'* (John 20:9; Luke 24:11.)

Even after Christ's final appearance 'some doubted' (Matthew 28:17). Jesus himself 'rebuked them for their lack of faith and their stubborn refusal to believe'. (Mark 16:14.) There is no picture here of imagination gone wild creating a glowing picture of victory to satisfy pious hope. To sceptical moods, exalted visions do not come. Nor do men seeking to deceive others confess to sadness, despair, fear, unbelief and astonishment.

Of course, faith came at last. Then hope, expanding. Then limitless joy. Finally readiness to die rather than deny.

Out of crushed, beaten-down men grew the most powerful force known to history. The very violence of Rome's reaction is evidence that the Empire feared the impact of its power on her very foundations.

Truth outstrips invention. They said they had seen the risen Christ. Their lives confirmed their words; and their violent, grisly deaths upheld the testimony of their lives. Fidelity to Christ has never been the soft option.

The cost of following Christ has always been high. But countless thousands have paid it.

A motiveless fraud would not have sustained the Church for two thousand years through attack, hostility and denial.

The Lord is risen indeed!

The destruction of death
and 'him that hath the power
of death', Satan, was made
certain that morning of
resurrection.

Paul expressed his highest
aim like this, *'That I may
know him and the power
of his resurrection. . . .'*
(Philippians 3:10, KJV.)

Because Christ rose,
we may rise – to the
risen life. In the risen
life sin's power is on
the wane. God offers
pardon and purity
together. Our sins
die with Christ and are
buried with him. Then,
with him, *we* must rise
again.

Through the Risen
Life we must remember
that we are not our
own; our eyes, our ears,
our hands, our feet, our
mind are his, and we
are under the weightiest
obligation possible to
use them to his honour
and glory.

Because he died for us,
this weighty obligation is
our highest joy. The Risen
Life involves studying God's
viewpoint about everything,
and, through the Spirit's
power, applying it in our
lives. It is continual
communion with him. It
is growth to maturity in
Jesus Christ and the power
of his Spirit.

The power of the Spirit yields fruit in the Risen Life. The *gifts* of the Spirit are divided unequally among believers; but *every* Risen Life, *all* born-again believers are expected to have *all* the *fruits* of the Spirit. As these fruits become apparent the Risen Life believer bears 'the family resemblance of the Son' (Romans 8:29, JBP).

The fruits of the Spirit as outlined in Galatians 5:22, 23 are love and eight facets of love: joy, peace, patience, gentleness, goodness, faithfulness, meekness and self-control.

Love

About love and the Risen
Life John writes, *'The way we
know we've been transferred
from death to life is that we
love our brothers and sisters.
Anyone who doesn't love is
as good as dead.'*
(1 John 3:14, MGE.)

Joy

The joy of the Spirit is indestructible.

'No one will take away your joy' (John 16:22).

The joy of the Christian is not dependent on circumstances or even environment.

Peace

The 'shalom' peace
of the Spirit contains
the idea of unity,
completeness, rest,
ease and security.

Patience

The patience of the Christian
endures ill treatment without
anger or thought of retaliation
or revenge.

Gentleness

The gentleness of the Spirit
pervades the whole of the
Christian's nature, banishing
all that is harsh and austere.
This gentleness is love
enduring.

Goodness

Goodness is love in action. It implies far more than simply 'doing good'. This goodness is thoroughgoing!

Faithfulness

Faithfulness is dependability:
one of the surest tests of a
Risen Life. The old nature can
counterfeit some of the fruit of
the Spirit but not this one.

Meekness

Meekness is not weakness. It means not timid, but *tamed*. Tamed like a wild horse brought under control. A river under control can be used to generate power.

Self-control

Perhaps, more accurately,
Spirit-controlled. This is the
Greek word for strong, able to
control thoughts and actions.
Self-control as a fruit of the
Spirit is the normal Christian
life taking its exercise.

The contrast between *works* and *fruit* is important. A machine in a factory *works*, and turns out a product, but it could never manufacture *fruit*. Fruit must grow out of life, and, in the case of the believer, it is the life of the Spirit (Galatians 5:25).

When you think of 'works' you think of effort, labour, strain and toil. When you think of 'fruit' you think of beauty, quietness, the unfolding of life. The flesh produces 'dead works' (Hebrews 9:14, KJV), but the Spirit produces living fruit.

And this living fruit has in it the seed for still more fruit. Love begets more love! Joy helps to produce more joy! Jesus is concerned that we produce 'fruit . . . more fruit . . . much fruit' (John 15:2, 5).

Jesus is alive, accessible,
our contemporary.

He is accessible through
prayer.

For this reason Christianity
will always be far more than
a mere philosophy or a
sentiment-soaked memory.

Christianity must ever be a living relationship with a living Lord: sitting at his feet, walking by his side, kneeling in his presence, facing up to life and all that life may throw at us in the knowledge that all power in Heaven and Earth is his – and that he will be with us always, even to the end of the world.
(Matthew 28:18-20.)

Commissioned by Jesus to go to the ends of the earth with his Gospel, the apostles were empowered by the descent of the Holy Spirit in the upper room. This empowerment took place at the Feast of Pentecost.

At Pentecost the priests presented the first loaves of the new harvest before God. The fullness of the year was gathered in.

Because travelling conditions were at their best, Jerusalem was never more crowded than for Pentecost.

The crowd to whom
Peter preached his
Pentecost sermon
would have numbered
hundreds of thousands
and come from many
lands.

The three crosses had been taken down. The tomb was empty for all to see. They had seen the wounds in hands, feet, side. From a high point on the Mount of Olives Jesus had visibly ascended.

Part of the post-Pentecost empowerment was that the apostles now had a Friend in high places.

With the power of the Spirit and Gospel truth burning inside them, the disciples could face the magistrate, the provincial governor, even Caesar himself. An all-conquering faith is more than enough to confront magic, witchcraft and paganism.

It was a singing
faith with which to
encounter imprisonment,
fire, sword and lions.
It was a glorious faith –
enough to outface
death, and the father
of terrors himself.

Beside the eternal throne of power, judgement and destiny stood Jesus, their Friend *(stands Jesus, our Friend)*, a merciful High Priest, 'touched with the feeling of our infirmities' (Hebrews 4:15, KJV), Advocate with the Father, only Mediator between man and God.

Even that was not all that
made hearts leap as the
early campaigners for Christ
embarked upon their mission.
Following the ascension
heavenly messengers had
echoed a promise repeated
many times by Jesus himself:
*'This same Jesus, which is
taken up from you into
heaven, shall so come in
like manner as you have seen
him go . . .'* (Acts 1:11, KJV).

This same Jesus –

Who had lain among the sharp
straws of a Bethlehem manger,
who had taught sublime truths
in the synagogue, who had
healed bodies and minds by
the inland sea, who had taken
a little child upon his knee . . .

They would see him again!

Even before the New Testament was written, when the Church gathered around the Lord's table to 'show the Lord's death till he come', their greeting (untranslated from the mother tongue of Christianity) was 'Maranatha': 'Lord, come!'

They would recall the words of their glorified Lord: *'Blessed are those servants, whom the master, when he comes, will find watching: . . . Therefore you also be ready, for the Son of man is coming at an hour you do not expect.'* (Luke 12:37, 40, NKJV.)

By Galilee Jesus shared a last
moment of intimacy with his
disciples.

When day dawned they'd recognised
him by the seashore and responded
to his invitation, 'Come and dine'. He
had built a fire by the water's edge and
cooked a fish breakfast. The prints of
the nails in his hands and feet were
clearly visible in the dawn light;
and the conquest of death he had
accomplished, and the empty tomb
he left behind, salvation, sweet peace,
unbounded joy and Heaven were on
offer to all men.

That was, at once, their message and their hope. Those who grasp what he offers with the empty hand of faith will hear his voice saying, 'Come and dine', and, like the eleven, meet him again on the shores of another sea: the sea of glass whose placid waters are red with the mingled fire of an eternal sunrise.

Face to face

Face to face with Christ my
   Saviour,
Face to face (what will it be)
When with rapture I behold
him,
Jesus Christ who died for me?

Only faintly now I see him,
With the darkling veil
between;

But a blessèd day is coming
When his glory shall be seen.

Face to face! Oh blissful
  moment!
Face to face – to see and
  know;
Face to face with my
  Redeemer,
Jesus Christ who loves me so.

Carrie Breck

'What shall I do?'

At a pivotal point in the trial of Jesus the Roman governor asked the mob, ' *"What shall I do, then, with Jesus who is called Christ?"* ' (Matthew 27:22). The mob roared, ' *"Crucify him!"* '

Albert Simpson wrote these poignant verses based on the Roman governor's question.

Jesus is standing in Pilate's hall,
Friendless, forsaken, betrayed by all;
Hearken! What meaneth the sudden
  call?
What will you do with Jesus?

What will you do with Jesus?
Neutral you cannot be;
Some day your heart will be asking,
'What will he do with me?'

Jesus is standing on trial still,
You can be false to him if you will,
You can be faithful through good or ill:
What will you do with Jesus?

What will you do with Jesus?
Neutral you cannot be;
Some day your heart will be asking,
'What will he do with me?'

Will you evade him as Pilate tried?
Or will you choose him, whate'er
    betide?
Vainly you struggle from him to hide:
What will you do with Jesus?

What will you do with Jesus?
Neutral you cannot be;
Some day your heart will be asking,
'What will he do with me?'

Will you, like Peter, your Lord deny?
Or will you scorn from his foes to fly?
Daring for Jesus to live or die?
What will you do with Jesus?

What will you do with Jesus?
Neutral you cannot be;
Some day your heart will be asking,
'What will he do with me?'

'Jesus, I give thee my heart today!
Jesus, I'll follow thee all the way,
Gladly obeying thee!' will you say:
'This I will do with Jesus!'

What will you do with Jesus?
Neutral you cannot be;
Some day your heart will be asking,
'What will he do with me?'

The writers of the four gospels set out bluntly the claims of Jesus to be the Christ, the Messiah, God's Son.

Jesus is the only man who ever lived who claimed to be God yet was judged sane by his wisest contemporaries.

Confucius did not claim to be God, nor did Zoroaster, nor did Buddha, nor did Mohammed. They had too much regard for their credibility for that. C. S. Lewis was right with regard to the claims of Jesus. . . .

Lewis said that, given the claims of Jesus, Jesus had to be mad or bad – or God. No one, apparently, is suggesting that he was mad or bad. True enough, some have made the claim that he was 'Simply a great teacher' . . .

But how could
he have been –
making such
claims? He did
not leave us that
option. He did
not intend to.

No single person has so changed the course of history, has been so loved and so despised, so hated and so adored, has so turned the bad into the good, the ugly into the beautiful – as Jesus of Nazareth.

Everywhere he went
people murmured,
'What sort of man is
this? Who is this?'
But Pilate was the
one who asked the
right question. . . .

'What shall I do, then, with Jesus who is called Christ?'

In a lifetime we may ask ourselves that question only once.

Everything in what remains of Time, and in Eternity, depends upon our answer.

'It is by grace you have been saved, through faith – and this not from yourselves, it is the gift of God . . .'
Ephesians 2:8

The word 'grace' is a kind of shorthand for the whole sum of unmerited blessings which come to us through Christ.

'. . . not by works, so that no one can boast. For we are God's workmanship . . .'
Ephesians 2:9

We are *God's* masterpieces. Salvation is not something we achieve. Believe, receive – and be free in Jesus.

*'If we confess our sins, he
is faithful and just and will
forgive us our sins and purify
us from all unrighteousness.'*
1 John 1:9

God both forgives and purifies
– remits our debt *and*
removes the stain.

The frustrating thing about time is that it always moves forward. There is no reverse gear. The hands on the clock always move clockwise. Therefore a deed once done can never be undone. A word once said can never be unsaid.

Only the blood of Christ can remove them from our hearts and send them as far from us as the East is from the West.